CROCHETED AND STITCHED JEWELLERY

CROCHETED AND STITCHED JEWELLERY

25 step-by-step projects

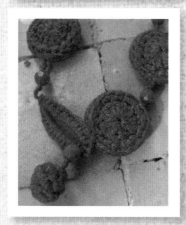

EMI IWAKIRI

CICO BOOKS

LONDON NEW YORK

Published in 2011 by CICO Books
An imprint of Ryland Peters & Small
20–21 Jockey's Fields, London WC1R 4BW
www.cicobooks.com

10 9 8 7 6 5 4 3 2 1

The projects in this book were originally published by CICO Books
in *Beautiful Hand-Stitched Jewellery*.

A CIP catalogue record for this book is available from the British Library.

ISBN 978-1-907563-75-1

Printed in China

Editor: Katie Hardwicke
Designer: Fahema Khanam
Photographer: Becky Maynes
Stylists: Nic Jottkandt and Sue Rowlands
Illustrator: Stephen Dew

Contents

Introduction

I really love handicrafts, as I can express my love to people through my work. I feel as though my heart itself is delivered to people with the things I make. I worked as a stylist for commercial photographers and as a designer of fashion clothing for a long time, and I loved and enjoyed my job, but it was a very busy and tiring world. I hoped to make things with which I could express myself and wanted to see the faces of people who wore and enjoyed my work. So, one day, I decided to leave and establish my own studio, and I haven't regretted my decision for one moment! I now enjoy my life as a crafter and a designer. I plan to move my studio to one of the southern islands of Japan – it is a beautiful island with a coral reef and a lot of greenery and flowers. I can always get inspiration for my designs from nature.

Crochet and fabric accessories are wonderful things to fill your wardrobe. They are versatile and help you to express your own sense of fashion. I hope you enjoy making these accessories and jewellery pieces with love, whether they are for your family, friends or yourself. I believe that you can feel the link with people and nature with a piece of thread.

Emi Iwakiri

I feel you are delighted,
I see you are smiling,
I listen to you humming,
To get my work of a piece of thread.

Rain makes plants fine,
Wind brings great energy,
Land nurtures them gently,
They can bloom towards the Sun.
Everything links with a piece of thread.

Even a tiny flower can make people happy,
You can do it with a piece of thread.

Embroidered
Key Ring

Vibrant Beaded
Collar

The projects in this chapter use straightforward sewing skills to create a range of exciting and individual pieces. With a few simple embroidery stitches and using beads and yarns as embellishments, you can create some very personal adornments that will bring colour, style and texture to your jewellery collection.

CHAPTER 1
Hand-Stitched Jewellery

Silk Pearl Necklace

Woollen Pearl Necklace

Elastic Knot Necklace

Musical Notes Necklace

Embroidered Necklace

Embroidered Bracelet

Embroidered Key Ring

Pompom Bracelet

Cashmere Flower Bracelet

Mini Cashmere Flower Necklace

Linen Flower Necklace

Linen Flower Hair Clip

Vibrant Beaded Collar

Silk Pearl Necklace

Silk and pearls are every girl's favourite! This fantastic necklace combines the two, creating 'pearl' beads from silk, simply strung together to give you a versatile necklace that would look stunning with an elegant dress, or hip and understated with designer jeans. You can use any colour of silk, but pearls in white, cream, black and red will look stylish against any outfit.

MATERIALS

½m (½yd) silk fabric,
cream or colour of your choice

Embroidery needle

Pearl cotton embroidery thread
No. 8, to match the silk fabric

Wadding

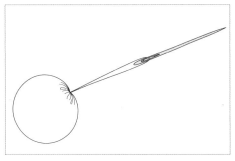

1 Cut out a 5-cm (2-in) square of silk and sew a circle 3.5cm (1½in) in diameter in running stitch in the centre. Fold up the edges and stuff the centre with wadding. Pull the thread to close the opening tightly and oversew the opening, trimming the excess thread. Make up 80 'pearl' beads in this manner.

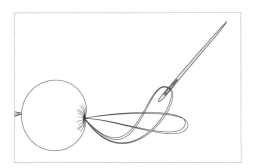

2 To join the beads, thread a needle with double thread. Push the needle through the centre of the first bead and tie a knot to secure it. Stitch through the fabric, make a loop in the thread, then pull the needle through to form a knot.

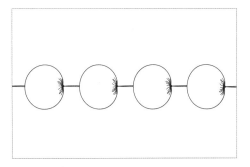

3 Leave a 5mm (¼in) space between pearls, ensuring that the space is never more than 1cm (½in), and continue to join the pearls, knotting closely to the pearl each time to keep them in place. Attach a ring clasp to the end (see page 85) and secure over a pearl to complete the necklace.

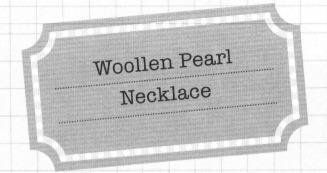

Woollen Pearl Necklace

MATERIALS

Old fine wool sweater

Pearl cotton embroidery thread No. 8, to match the sweater

Embroidery needle

This is a great way to recycle loved but worn sweaters – this simple project uses strips cut from a fine wool sweater to create a woolly version of the pearl necklace. Any fine knit sweater would work well – especially one in variegated colours. Thick or hand-knitted sweaters are not suitable.

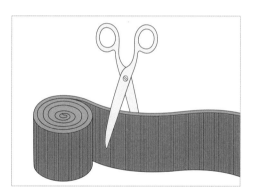

1 Cut the sweater into 1-cm (½-in) wide strips, across the width, parallel to the stitches. Roll the strip into a ball, approximately 1.5cm (¾in) in diameter. Trim the excess strip.

2 Sew the edges together, securing the top and bottom ends to make a ball (see step 1, page 11). Repeat to make 73 wool balls in total. To make the clasp ring, wind the embroidery thread five or six times around a ball to make the loops. Sew around the loops in blanket stitch (see page 86). Join the clasp ring and beads together with a length of embroidery thread, knotting before and after each bead (see step 3, page 11).

Elastic Knot Necklace

This is the perfect accessory for any busy working woman's wardrobe! You can use it with a navy business suit on Monday, a grey sweater on Tuesday, a good companion for a business trip on Wednesday and Thursday, and with a little black dress for a date on Friday! As this is made of elastic, it is very light and comfortable to wear – you can enjoy it as a single necklace, a double choker and a hair accessory.

MATERIALS

6m (6½yd) elastic cord

Stranded embroidery thread in different colours

Embroidery needle

Sewing thread

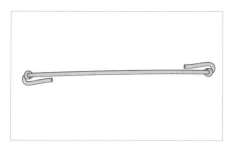

1 Cut the elastic cord into 49 lengths of 10cm (4in) and one piece of 1m (40in). Tie a knot at both ends of all the shorter lengths. Fold back the end of the cord.

2 Wind a length of embroidery thread around the knotted end of the cord, approximately 20–25 times, securing the start of the thread beneath the wrapped thread. Trim the end of the thread and tuck it inside the wrapped coil. Repeat the process around the knot at the other end of the elastic cord.

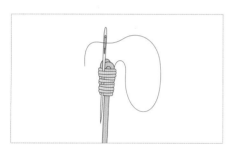

3 With sewing thread, secure the wrapped embroidery thread with a few stitches from the bottom to the top to hold it all in place. Repeat step 2 approximately five times to build up the knot. Repeat to complete all 49 pieces of elastic.

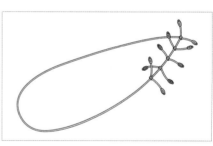

4 Repeat steps 2–3 on both ends of the longer length cord. Tie the shorter pieces of the cords along the length of the longer piece. Tie at the neck to secure.

Musical Notes Necklace

MATERIALS

1m (1yd) white cotton fabric

Embroidery needle

Pearl cotton embroidery thread No. 8, black

2.50mm crochet hook

Black seed beads

8mm Czech cut beads

Black bamboo or bugle beads

This fun necklace is embroidered with musical notes – I feel as though music is dancing around my neck whenever I wear it! Worn with a classic little black dress, it will look mischievous and charming.

Embroidery key for 5 designs

25mm (1in) 25mm (1in) 25mm (1in)

22mm (⅞in) 22mm (⅞in)

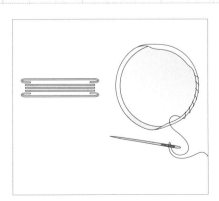

1 Cut out circles from the cotton fabric with the following diameters: for each large disc, cut two 26mm/1¹⁄₁₆in (A) and four 25mm/1in (B); for each small disc, cut two 23mm/¹³⁄₁₆in (C) and four 22mm/⅞in (D).

Cut out enough circles to make six large and eight small embroidered discs. Fold over the edges. For the larger discs, sandwich four pieces of B between two layers of A as padding. Whipstitch around them to complete the disc. For the smaller discs, sandwich four pieces of D between two layers of C and whipstitch together.

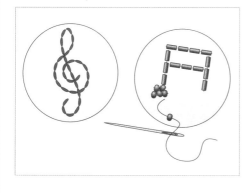

2 Embroider a motif on each disc following the embroidery key above. Use small seed beads combined with bamboo or bugle beads, and stitch each motif using a neat running stitch (see page 86). Repeat to make all the discs.

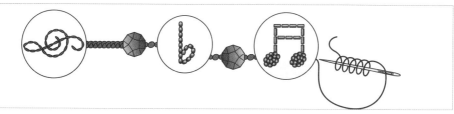

3 Take a large embroidered disc (the clef here), attach the thread through the top edge and knot to secure. Chain stitch (see page 88) approximately five chains, then thread on a bead and knot to secure. Attach the thread to a small disc. Push through and out the opposite side, off centre. Knot the thread by wrapping the thread around the needle several times, attach a bead, knot again and join to the next embroidered disc. Continue until all the embroidered discs are attached with an inner loop, finishing on the inner edge of the final disc. Bring the thread out on the centre of the outer edge of the last disc.

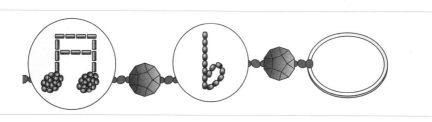

4 Attach a ring clasp (see page 85) at the end of the inside loop.

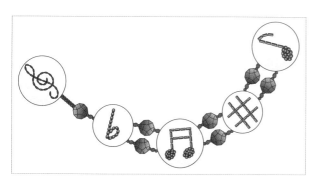

5 Repeat with an outer loop, attaching the beads and discs together as in step 3, starting from the inner edge of the last disc. As it is longer than the inside loop, adjust the balance with a few more knots in between discs.

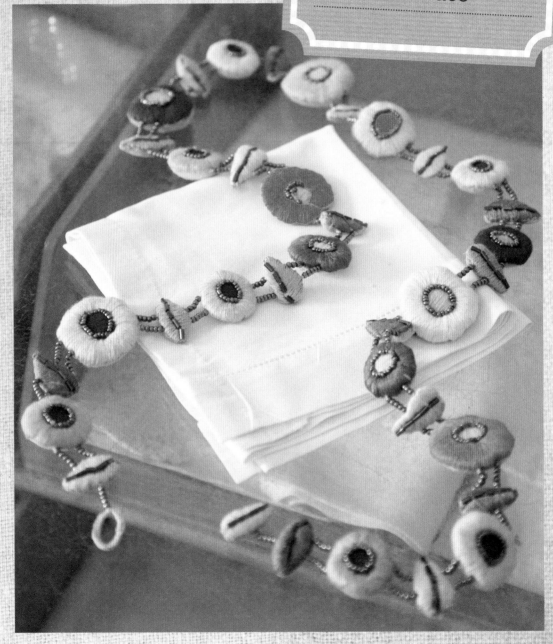

This necklace of embroidered flowers is a very impressive piece. For maximum impact, wear it with a simple top that will let the necklace take centre stage. Evoking the blooms of a summer courtyard garden, this beautiful piece would look equally stunning in a picture frame when you're not wearing it!

MATERIALS
2m (2½yd) cotton fabric
Embroidery needle
Stranded embroidery thread in
a selection of different colours
Fabric marker pen
Pearl cotton embroidery thread No. 8
Bronze seed beads
5mm green bugle beads
Bronze round beads

1 For each embroidered flower, cut out circles from the base fabric with the following diameters:
Large flowers: two 5cm/2in (A) and four 4cm/1¾in (B). Cut out enough for seven large flowers.
Small flowers: two 4cm/1¾in (C) and four 3cm/1½in (D). Cut out enough for 10 small flowers.

For each leaf, cut two 1.5cm/⅝in (E) long leaf shapes and four 1cm/½in (F) long leaf shapes. Cut out enough for 18 leaves.

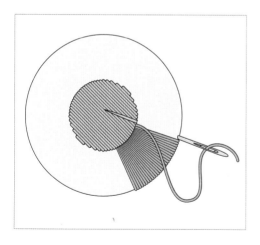

2 To make a large flower base, fold under the edges of each piece A. Sandwich four pieces of B between two of A, and whipstitch together. Repeat to make seven bases. Repeat with the small flower shapes, sandwiching four pieces of D between two of C, to make 10 flowers. Make 18 leaves in the same way. Embroider the flower base. Using a fabric marker pen, draw a circle 1.5cm (⅝in) in diameter in the centre of the base. Work satin stitch across the centre (see page 86). Work satin stitches in stranded embroidery thread around the edge in a contrasting colour for the petals.

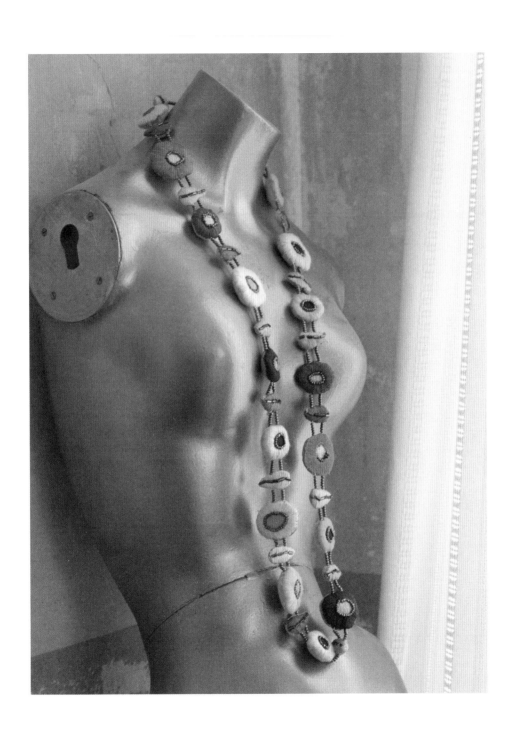

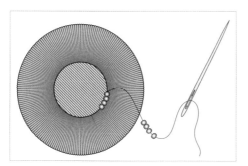

3 Thread four bronze seed beads onto a length of No. 8 embroidery thread and attach them around the centre of the flower. Repeat until you have completed the circle. Repeat to add beads to the centre of all the flowers.

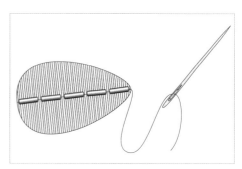

4 To complete the leaf, work straight stitches or satin stitch in stranded embroidery thread across the leaf, separating the right and the left at the centre of the leaf. Attach four or five bugle beads down the centre of the leaf.

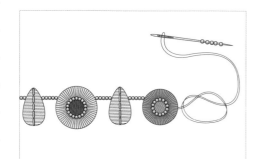

5 Join the flowers together in the following sequence: leaf, large flower, leaf, small flower. To join the flowers, thread a needle with No. 8 embroidery thread, string on approximately five small round beads, knot the thread, then take the needle through the leaf base and out on the opposite side. Tie a knot, then thread on five beads, knot the thread and attach a flower in the same way.

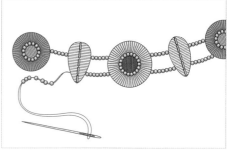

6 After the last leaf, make a ring clasp at the end of the inside loop (see page 85). Then add the outer necklace loop, adding six or seven beads between each flower and leaf to adjust the length of the loop.

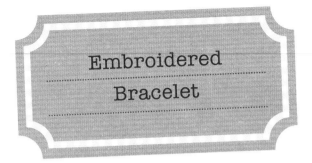

Embroidered Bracelet

MATERIALS

1m (1yd) cotton fabric

Fabric marker pen

Embroidery needle

Stranded embroidery thread in a selection of colours (fuchsia pink, pale pink, off-white, white, orange, light green)

Bronze seed beads

6mm pink Czech cut beads

5mm green bugle beads

The perfect complement to the long double-strand necklace on page 24, or fantastic on its own, this pretty bracelet combines a simple palette of colours with delicate pink faceted beads. This piece would be perfect with a floaty summer dress at cocktail hour.

1 For each embroidered flower, cut out circles from the base fabric with the following diameters: two 5cm/2in (A) and four 4cm/1¾in (B). Cut out enough for 10 flowers. Make each flower base following the instructions in step 2 on page 21. Embroider each flower with contrasting threads and attach small bronze beads to the centre, following the instructions in step 3 on page 22.

To make the leaf clasp, cut out two 1.5cm/⅝in long leaf shapes and four 1cm/½in long leaf shapes. Make the leaf following the instructions in step 4 on page 22.

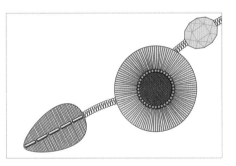

2 Attach the leaf to the flowers with a length of chain crochet (page 88), then join the flowers together with a loop of chain crochet, incorporating a Czech bead between each flower.

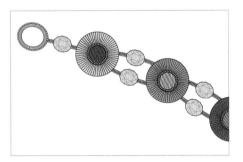

3 After the last flower, add a bead and make the end of the inside loop part of the ring clasp (see page 85). Add the outer necklace loop, adding beads between each flower and adding more chain stitches between the beads to adjust the length, if necessary.

Bring a tired handbag back to life with this stylish flower charm or key ring in soft yarns and vibrant colours. It can easily be adapted to hang from a belt loop, your mobile phone or even your dog's lead! Small and simple, it is a wonderful piece to make and give to your friends.

MATERIALS

1m (1yd) cotton fabric

Fabric marker pen

Embroidery needle

Stranded embroidery thread in a selection
of colours (fuchsia pink, pale pink, taupe,
orange, light green)

Bronze seed beads

Faceted beads

Small round beads

Large round beads

Two 8mm jump rings

Key ring or clasp

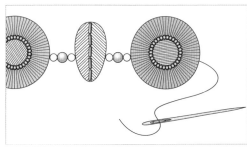

1 Make a base for each embroidered flower (three large and two small, see page 21), then embroider and embellish with beads (see steps 2–3 on pages 21–23). Make four leaf shapes following step 4 on page 23. Thread a needle and string on a faceted bead. Bring the needle out through the first flower, string on a small bead, a large bead and a small bead, then join through the centre of a leaf, bringing the needle out on the opposite side and stringing on beads in the same order. Join the flowers and leaves, attaching a faceted bead on the end of the last flower.

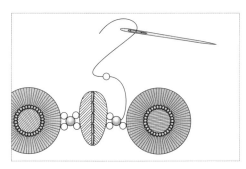

2 String the outer loop, adding a small bead, passing the needle through the large bead and stringing another small bead between the flower and leaf.

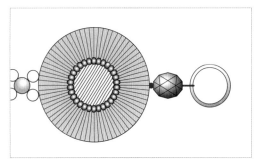

3 Bring the thread through the faceted bead and attach a jump ring to each end by threading on the jump ring, bringing the needle back through the bead and knotting to secure. Attach a clasp or key ring to the jump rings.

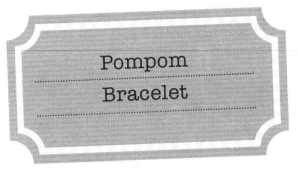

Pompom
Bracelet

MATERIALS

DK yarn in several colours

3mm crochet hook

Metal bracelet, 7cm (2¾in) in diameter

Needle and beading thread

Bronze seed beads

This fun pompom bracelet brings to mind a circus costume or a folk tambourine. I love to wear several bracelets together, with a gradation of colours from yellow to orange, pink to purple, green to blue, and pale grey to dark grey. A single bracelet with multicoloured pompoms looks modern and striking. However you use them, making the downy pompoms is an enjoyable job.

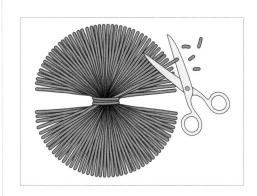

1 Make seven pompoms with a diameter of approximately 2.5cm (1in), in different coloured yarns (see page 85). Tie yarn to bracelet. Work dc over bracelet until it is covered. Fasten off. Sew in ends, joining first dc to last dc. (See step 2 on page 48.)

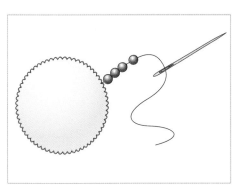

2 Thread a needle with beading thread and push it through the centre of a pompom. Thread on four or five seed beads.

3 Take the needle through the edge of the crochet and sew it in place with a double knot, then take the thread back through the beads and secure the thread in the pompom. Attach the remaining six pompoms equidistantly around the bracelet. Make several bracelets in different colours to wear together.

Cashmere Flower Bracelet

Give your cherished but worn cashmere sweaters a new life as beautiful flowers (see pages 81–83). With elasticated thread, this bracelet fits snugly to your wrist and is very comfortable and cosy on a chilly day. Match the colours to your winter coat or woolly cardigan and you will be ready to face any weather in style.

MATERIALS

Embroidery needle

6mm stretched waxed thread

Four rolled flowers (see page 82)

Four eight-petalled flowers
(see page 83)

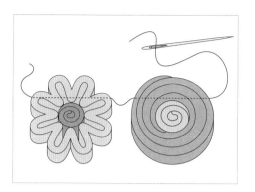

1 Thread a needle with stretch waxed thread. Push the needle through the upper portion of a flower, approximately 1cm (½in) from the top, and then through a roll at the same place. Repeat to join four flowers and four rolls alternately. Knot the thread to secure.

2 Push the needle though the lower portion of the flower approximately 1cm (½in) from the base and attach it to a rolled flower. Continue to join the flowers together. Knot the thread to secure at the end.

3 To complete the bracelet, tie the thread ends together with a knot.

Mini Cashmere Flower Necklace

MATERIALS

Embroidery needle

Elastic yarn No. 30 (thick)

Old cashmere sweaters, in
a selection of different colours

Pearl cotton embroidery thread No. 8,
red or to tone with the sweaters

This long necklace is very easy to string together and you can adjust the length by simply adding or reducing the number of flowers. Don't feel that you have to wear this in the conventional way – tied loosely around your waist, it looks great as a belt, too!

1 Make 39 small petalled flowers (see pages 81 and 83), using cord A: 8mm x 6cm (⅜in x 2¼in), cord B: 1.8mm x 13.5cm (¹⁄₁₆in x 5¼in). Create flowers in three colourways.

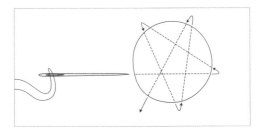

2 Make a ball using a strip of wool 1cm x 7cm (½in x 2¾in). Stitch through the ball in a zigzag to maintain its shape. Make a ring clasp with two or three loops of yarn with a diameter slightly larger than the ball (see page 85).

3 Thread a needle with double embroidery thread. Push the needle through the base of the ring clasp and tie the thread in a double knot. Push the needle through a petal and the centre of the flower and make a knot in the thread.

4 Take the needle out through a petal and attach the next flower following the instructions in step 2, leaving a length of approximately 1.5cm (⅝in) between each flower.

5 Attach the ball to the last flower, securing with a double knot and leaving a 5mm (¼in) length of thread between the flower and the ball.

Linen Flower Necklace

The frayed edges of the flowers make a fashionable accent in this statement necklace – you won't need any other accessories. Try different colourways: black linen with multicoloured beads is dramatic and strong, and with black beads is chic; white linen with multicoloured beads looks cute, and with white beads is very elegant. You can easily extend the pattern to make an unusual belt, too.

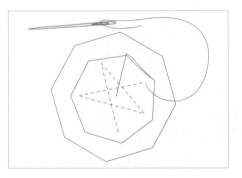

1 Copy the templates on page 91 to make card templates and cut out 12 pieces of each hexagonal shape in linen and four pieces of the leaf shape. Place B on A. Make a tuck across the centre of B and tack to A with random stitches. Repeat to make 11 more petals.

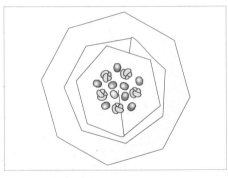

2 Place C on B, make a tuck and attach to the two layers with small stitches. Embroider five French knots (see page 86) randomly in the centre of a flower. Embroider some seeds beads around them. Make 11 more flowers.

MATERIALS
½m (½yd) linen
Embroidery needle
Pearl cotton embroidery thread
No. 8, beige
Multicoloured seed beads
Delica beads

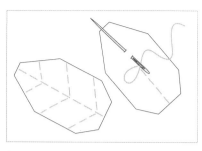

3 Sew two leaf shapes together (right) and embroider running stitches to represent the leaf veins (left).

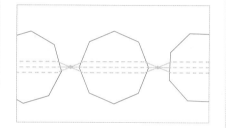

4 Join the flowers together using triple running stitches on the reverse of the larger petal (A) only, making a knot between flowers. Be careful not to sew onto the top two layers, avoiding the stitches showing through.

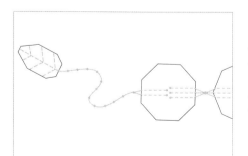

5 Stop the stitches and make a knot to secure at the centre of the last flower. Sew double running stitches from the centre to the edge of the last flower. Bring the two threads together and make knots at 1.5cm (⅝in) intervals along a 17cm (6½in) length. Join the end leaf to the threads. Repeat to attach the leaf at the other end.

Linen Flower
Hair Clip

This linen flower hair accessory will perfectly complement the necklace on page 34, but it's striking enough to work as a single accessory. You could also attach the flower to a brooch pin for an informal corsage, which can then be attached to a blazer or a bag.

MATERIALS

Linen

Embroidery needle

Pearl cotton embroidery thread
No. 8, beige

Multicoloured seed beads

Delica beads

Hair slide or brooch pin

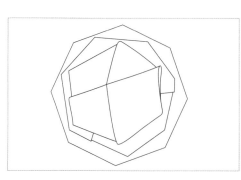

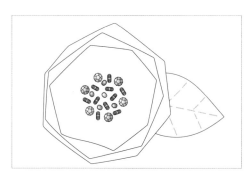

1 Copy the templates on pages 92–93 and make card templates. Cut out two pieces of the hexagonal and leaf shapes from fabric. Place B on A and make two tucks in B. Place C on B and make four tucks in C. Pin in place.

2 Thread double embroidery yarn through the needle and layer the two leaf shapes, sewing leaf veins in place following the instructions in step 3 on page 35. Sew the petals and leaf together on the reverse, taking care not to show the stitches on the upper side. Hide the stitches inside tucks on petal C. Work 10 French knots (see page 86) and attach seed beads in the centre of the flower. Sew larger beads around them. Attach a barrette or brooch pin to the back.

Vibrant Beaded Collar

MATERIALS

15-cm (6-in) square quilted beige linen

15-cm (6-in) square beige linen for lining

Pearl cotton embroidery thread No. 8, to match

Selection of beads, such as seed beads, large cut beads, round beads, flat beads

Made from a heavy linen, this luxurious collar, embellished with an array of sparkling beads, will bring instant glamour to any outfit. Perfect for evening wear, it will also look impressive against a plain-knit sweater and jeans.

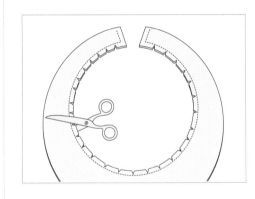

1 Photocopy the template on page 90 at 200%. Use the paper template as a pattern to cut out two necklace base shapes from the quilted linen and the lining. Place right sides together and sew a 5mm (¼in) seam across the ends and around the inner circle. Carefully snip into the curve to ease the seam.

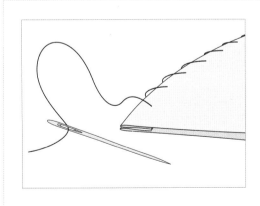

2 Turn right sides out and press the stitched seam carefully to form a smooth curve. Turn under the outer edge to the wrong side by 1cm (½in) on the top and base. Press, then hand stitch together and press again.

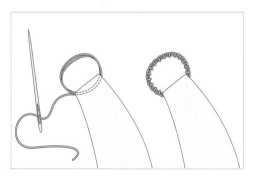

3 Thread a needle with embroidery thread and make a ring clasp (see page 85) along the end of one side.

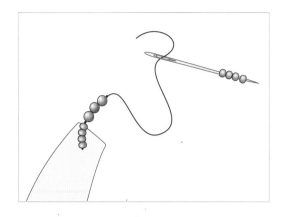

4 Make the catch on the opposite edge. Thread a needle and bring it out about 2cm (¾in) inside from the edge and work a French knot (see page 85). Thread four seed beads onto the thread and make a knot. Thread on three round beads, make a knot and thread four seed beads. Sew a few stitches and make a knot to secure, then cut off the thread.

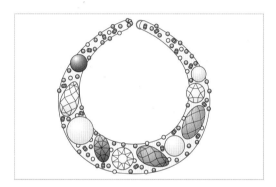

5 Attach beads to the base, taking care not to show the stitches on the reverse. Sew the larger stones in place first, then the smaller stones and add a few French knots or bullion knots, or other decorative stitches.

6 Attach the beads to the edge, starting with the central bead in the middle of the necklace and then adding a bead alternately on the left and right, judging the distance between the beads by eye. Bringing the needle out from the back of the hem at the base, thread on two round beads, a teardrop bead and a round bead. Bring the thread back through the teardrop bead and a round bead, and sew a knot at the hem to secure. Bring the needle out approximately 2.5cm (1in) along to attach the next bead. Repeat to attach 11 hanging beads in total.

Muted Beaded Collar

With an understated colour palette, this variation on the Vibrant Beaded Collar on page 38 looks cool and chic. Simply follow steps 1–3 on page 39, then follow the instructions on the right, using beads in neutral and brown tones.

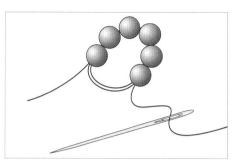

Make a catch as a part of clasp on the other side of the bases. Bring the needle out about 2cm (¾in) inside from the edge and work a French knot. Thread six round beads and bring the thread through the beads twice before making a knot and securing. Embellish the necklace base shape with your chosen design (see steps 5–6 on page 40).

MATERIALS

15-cm (6-in) square quilted beige linen

15-cm (6-in) square beige linen for lining

Pearl cotton embroidery thread No. 8, to match

Selection of beads, such as large cut beads, round beads, flat beads, teardrop beads

Bridal Flower
Necklace

These projects use a few basic crochet stitches to create some beautifully-textured pieces of jewellery. From simple, embellished rings to the delicate cascade of flowers fit for a bride, there are projects to suit all levels of ability. Using wool, silk, cotton and raffia, the variations are endless and you will soon find many other uses for the flowers, chains and crosses that you create.

CHAPTER 2
Crocheted
Jewellery

Cotton Flower
Ring

This simple necklace makes a bold accent on T-shirts or a linen dress in summer with the strong colours of the raffia yarns glowing in the sunshine. A flower clasp is a very charming part of the necklace – you can enjoy it at the front or the back.

CROCHET KEY

ch (chain stitch)	O
dc (double crochet)	✕
ss (slip stitch)	●
tr (treble crochet)	┼
2dc in same st	⋎

MATERIALS

Rayon raffia yarn, in red, pink and orange

4mm crochet hook

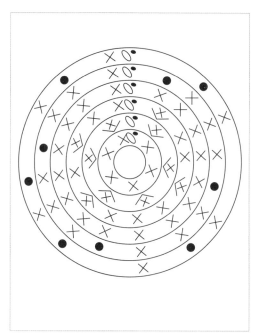

1 Large beads:

Make 2ch.

Round 1 1 6dc in second ch from hook, ss in 1ch.

Round 2 1ch, 2dc in each dc, ss in 1ch. 12dc.

Round 3 1ch, 1dc in first dc, [1dc in next dc, 2dc in next dc] twice, 1dc in each of next 3dc, 2dc in next dc, 1dc in each of next 2dc, 2dc in last dc, ss in 1ch. 16dc.

Round 4 1ch, 1dc in each dc, ss in 1ch.

Round 5 1ch, [1dc in each of 3dc, miss 1dc] 4 times, ss in 1ch. 12dc.

Round 6 1ch, [1dc in dc, miss 1dc] 6 times, ss in 1ch. 6dc.

Cut yarn, thread end through front loop of each dc, pull tight to close hole. Fasten off securely.

Make 16 large beads in assorted shades.

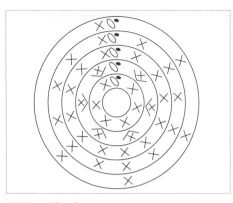

2 Bead clasp:

Make 2ch.

Round 1 6dc in second ch from hook, ss in 1ch.

Round 2 1ch, 2dc in each dc, ss in 1ch. 12dc.

Round 3 1ch, 1dc in each dc, ss in 1ch.

Round 4 1ch, 1dc in each dc, ss in 1ch.

Round 5 1ch, [1dc in dc, miss 1dc] 6 times, ss in 1ch. 6dc.

Cut yarn, thread end through front loop of each dc, pull tight to close hole. Fasten off securely.

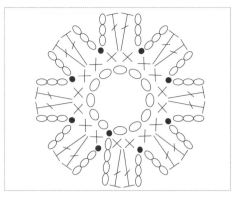

3 Flower clasp:

Make 12ch, ss in first ch to form a ring.

Round 1 1ch, 16dc in ring, ss in first ch.

Round 2 [3ch, 2tr in next dc, 3ch, ss in next dc] 8 times, ss in first ch.

Fasten off.

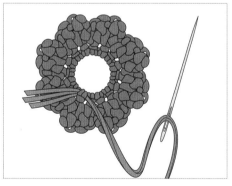

4 Thread a tapestry needle with a 1m (1¼yd) length of yarn and secure through a stitch on the reverse of the flower clasp.

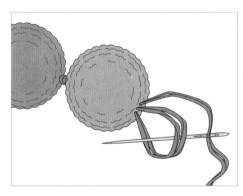

5 Push the needle through the centre of a large bead and knot to secure. Alternating colours, continue until all beads are joined, ending with bead clasp. Push needle back through bead clasp and fasten off securely. Push bead clasp through hole in centre of flower clasp to fasten necklace.

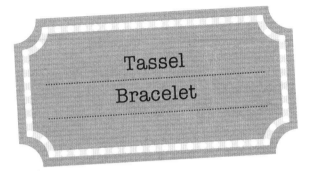

Tassel
Bracelet

MATERIALS

DK yarn in a selection of colours

3mm crochet hook

Metal bracelet

Length of clear nylon
beading thread

Bronze seed beads

The inspiration for these designs came from the cowgirls of the Wild West. I like to wear three bracelets together, in different colours. Your choice of yarn is important – a cotton yarn is light and summery; a wool yarn is warm and rich, perfect for accessorizing autumn and winter knits. While they look fantastic together, each piece makes a bold statement on its own – just remember to wear them with a fringed suede skirt and boots!

CROCHET KEY

ss (slip stitch)	●
ch (chain stitch)	O
dc (double crochet)	✕

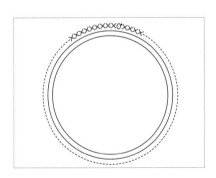

1 Make seven 4cm (1½in) tassels in different coloured yarns with contrasting bands (see page 84). Thread a needle with beading thread and attach to tassel above contrasting band. Thread on enough beads to fit around tassel and join to form a ring. Take needle under contrasting band and work another ring of beads. Fasten off securely.

2 Tie yarn to bracelet. Work dc over bracelet until it is covered. Fasten off. Sew in ends, joining first dc to last dc.

3 Thread a needle with beading thread, attach to the bracelet and thread on five small beads. Push the needle through the top of a tassel, bring the thread back through the beads and secure neatly to the bracelet. Attach the remaining six tassels equidistantly around the bracelet. Make two more bracelets, either in matching or contrasting colours, and wear together or separately.

Crocheted Discs Necklace

Some islands are surrounded by pink coral and so have pink beaches. I used genuine pink coral beads for this necklace, imagining it would transport me to a southern island, with the waves breaking on the pink sand. This piece would look great with a vintage lace blouse or dress.

MATERIALS	CROCHET KEY	
Pearl cotton embroidery thread No. 5, red	ss (slip stitch)	●
2mm crochet hook	ch (chain stitch)	O
Embroidery needle	dc (double crochet)	×
15 cut coral beads	tr (treble crochet)	⊤
	2dc in same st	⋎

1 Bead:
Round 1 Wrap yarn around finger to form a ring, 3ch, 11tr in ring, ss in top of 3ch.
Round 2 1ch, 1dc in same place as ss, [2dc in next tr, 1dc in next tr] 5 times, 2dc in last tr, ss in 1ch.
Fasten off. Make a total of 28 beads.

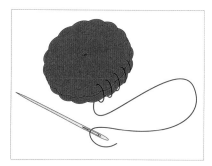

2 With wrong sides together, sew beads together in pairs joining through stitches of round 2.
Make 14 double beads.

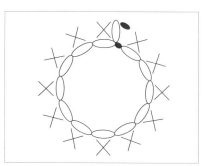

3 Clasp ring:

Make 12ch, ss in first ch to form a ring.
Round 1 1ch, 12dc in ring, ss in 1ch.
Fasten off.

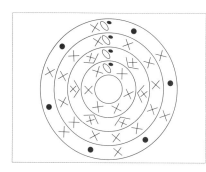

4 Clasp ball:

Round 1 Wrap yarn around finger to form a ring, 1ch, 6dc in ring, ss in 1ch.
Round 2 1ch, 2dc in each dc, ss in 1ch, 12dc.
Round 3 1ch, 1dc in each dc, ss in 1ch.
Round 4 1ch, [1dc in next dc, miss next dc] 6 times, ss in 1ch.
Fasten off.

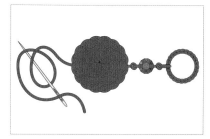

5 Thread a needle with embroidery thread and secure end to clasp ring.
*Make a knot, thread on a coral bead, make a knot, thread on a double bead pushing needle from edge to edge through centre of double bead, repeat from * until all double beads are threaded, make a knot, thread on a coral bead, make a knot and attach clasp ball.
Fasten off securely.

Flower Corsage

MATERIALS

4mm crochet hook

Rayon raffia yarn in pink, yellow and green

Brooch pin

This raffia corsage will add an accent of casual elegance to your wardrobe. A corsage is extremely versatile and shouldn't be worn only on special occasions – the sharp, modern lines of the petals bring a casual elegance to an everyday shirt. Try wearing several corsages together for a colourful bouquet effect!

CROCHET KEY

ss (slip stitch)	●
ch (chain stitch)	O
dc (double crochet)	×
htr (half treble crochet)	T
tr (treble crochet)	⊤̵
dtr (double treble crochet)	⊦̵

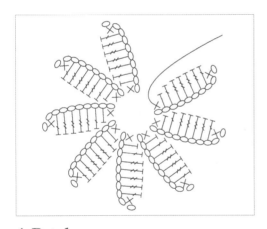

1 Petals:

Using pink, *make 10ch, 1dc in 2nd ch from hook. 1tr in next ch, 1dtr in each of next 4ch, 1tr in next ch, 1htr in next ch, 1dc in last ch, rep from * until a total of 8 petals have been worked.
Fasten off leaving a 60cm (24in) length of yarn.

2 With WS facing arrange petals to form a circle, overlapping petals. Catch ends tog at centre.

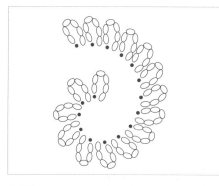

3 Flower centre:

Using yellow, *make 6ch, ss in first of 6ch,
rep from * until there are 16 loops.
Fasten off leaving a 20cm (8in) length of yarn.
Wind the length of loops round to form the
centre and sew tog on WS.

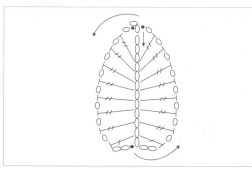

4 Leaf:

Using green, make 15ch, 1tr in 4th ch from hook, [1ch, 1dtr
in next ch] 7 times, 1ch, miss 3ch, 1ss, 1ch and 1ss in last
ch, working along other side of ch work 1ch, miss 3ch, [1dtr
in next ch, 1ch] 7 times, 1tr in next ch, 2ch, ss in next ch.
Fasten off.

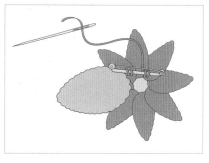

5 Place flower centre in middle of petals
and sew securely on WS. Sew end of leaf
to WS of flower. Sew brooch pin to WS
of flower.

MATERIALS

4mm crochet hook

Rayon raffia yarn, off-white, beige, brown

Brooch pin

In warm, toning colours, this corsage would also look lovely pinned to the ribbon of a summer straw hat or adding a touch of glamour to an everyday shopping basket. Experiment with colour combinations to see you through the seasons.

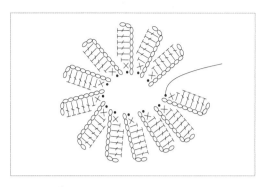

CROCHET KEY

ss (slip stitch)	●
ch (chain stitch)	O
dc (double crochet)	×
htr (half treble crochet)	T
tr (treble crochet)	Ŧ
dtr (double treble crochet)	Ŧ

1 Petals:

Using off white, *make 10ch, miss 2ch, 1tr in each of next 5ch, 1htr in next ch, 1dc in next ch, 1ss in last ch, rep from * until a total of 12 petals have been worked.

Fasten off leaving a 60cm (24in) length of yarn. With WS facing arrange petals to form a circle, overlapping petals. Catch ends tog at centre (see step 2, page 52).

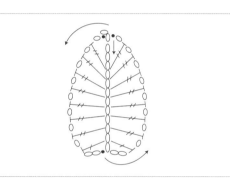

3 Leaf:

Using brown, make 15ch, 1tr in 4th ch from hook, [1ch, 1dtr in next ch] 7 times, 1ch, miss 3ch, 1ss, 1ch and 1ss in last ch, working along other side of ch work 1ch, miss 3ch, [1dtr in next ch, 1ch] 7 times, 1tr in next ch, 2ch, ss in next ch. Fasten off. Make a second leaf.

Place flower centre in middle of petals and sew securely on WS. Sew end of leaves to WS of flower. Sew brooch pin to WS of flower (see step 5, page 53).

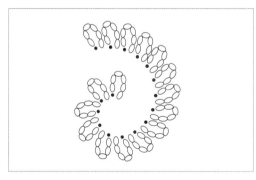

2 Flower centre:

Using beige, *make 6ch, ss in first of 6ch, rep from * until there are 16 loops.

Fasten off leaving a 20cm (8in) length of yarn. Wind the length of loops round to form the centre and sew tog on WS.

Cross Necklace

MATERIALS
3mm crochet hook
Fine Rayon raffia yarn,
off-white

Made entirely from raffia yarn, this necklace and bracelet
were inspired by an illustration from an antique book.
The key to the success of the piece is the shape of the
cross – it may take a little practice to get it right, but
be patient and you will be rewarded.

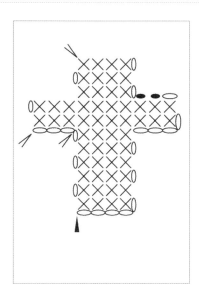

1 Cross:

Make 5ch.

Row 1 (RS)1dc in 2nd ch from hook, 1dc in each ch. 4dc.

Rows 2–6 1ch, 1dc in each of 4dc.

Join a short length of yarn to 1ch at start of row 6 and make 3ch. Fasten off.

Row 7 4ch, 1dc in 2nd ch from hook, 1dc in each of next 2ch, 1dc in each of next 4dc, 1dc in each of 3ch. 10dc.

Row 8 1ch, 1dc in each of 10dc.

Row 9 1ch, miss 1st dc, 1ss in each of next 2dc, 1ch, 1dc in each of next 4dc, turn. 4dc.

Rows 10–11 1ch, 1dc in each of 4dc.

Fasten off.

Make a 2nd cross.

With wrong sides tog, sew the 2 crosses tog around outer edges.

CROCHET KEY

ss (slip stitch)   ●

ch (chain stitch)   O

dc (double crochet)   ×

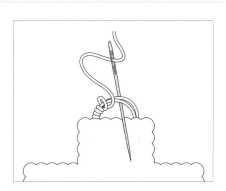

2 Sew a small loop at the centre of the top edge of the cross and cover the loop with whipstitch.

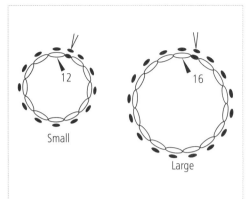

Small

12

16

Large

3 Chain 1:

Large ring Make 16ch, ss in 1st ch to join ring, 1ss in each ch, ss in 1st ss. Fasten off.

Small ring Make 12ch, thread end through large ring, ss in 1st ch to join ring, 1ss in each ch, ss in 1st ss. Fasten off.

Make and link a large ring to small ring.

*Make and link a small ring to last large ring.

Make and link a large ring to last small ring.

Rep from *, making and linking small and large rings alternately, until 23 large and 22 small rings are joined into a length.

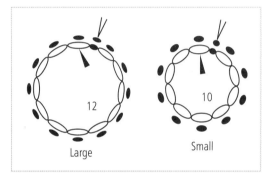

12

10

Large

Small

4 Chain 2, used for joining the cross:

Large ring Make 12ch, ss in 1st ch to join ring, 1ss in each ch, ss in 1st ss. Fasten off.

Small ring Make 10ch, thread end through large ring, ss in 1st ch to join ring, 1ss in each ch, ss in 1st ss. Fasten off.

Make and link large and small rings alternately until 9 large and 8 small rings are joined into a length, linking final large ring to both the last small ring and the centre large ring on chain 1.

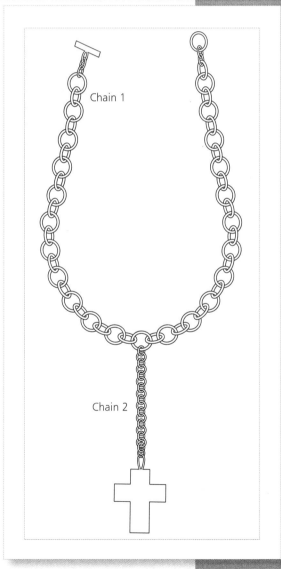

Chain 1

Chain 2

58 *Crocheted Jewellery*

5 Clasp:

Make 7ch, 1dc in 2nd ch from hook, 1dc in each ch. 6dc. Fasten off.
Sew a small loop at the centre of the top edge of the clasp and cover the loop with whipstitch (see step 2, page 57).

6 At one end of chain 1, make and link 2 small (10ch) rings and 1 large (12ch) ring. At other end, make and link 2 small (10ch) rings, also linking the second ring through the loop in the clasp.

7 Make 8ch, thread end through large ring at end of chain 2 and through the loop on the cross, ss in 1st ch to join ring, 1ss in each ch, ss in 1st ss. Fasten off.

MATERIALS

3mm crochet hook

Silk yarn, off-white, beige

Metallic yarn, gold

Needle

CROCHET KEY

ss (slip stitch)	•
ch (chain stitch)	O
dc (double crochet)	×
htr (half treble crochet)	T
tr (treble crochet)	Ŧ
dtr (double treble crochet)	Ŧ

Silk Flower Ring

The reflection of the white silk yarn used for this flower ring makes your skin look smooth and bright, infusing it with the power of beauty. The centre of the flower is in a slightly darker colour so that the flowers look three-dimensional.

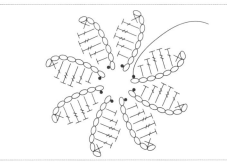

1 Petals:

Using off-white, *make 8ch, 1dc in 2nd ch from hook. 1tr in next ch, 1dtr in each of next 2ch, 1tr in next ch, 1htr in next ch, 1ss in last ch, rep from * until a total of 8 petals have been worked.
Fasten off leaving a 30cm (12in) length of yarn.

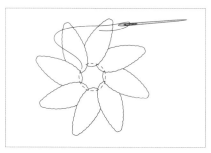

2 With WS facing arrange petals to form a circle, overlapping petals. Catch ends tog at centre.

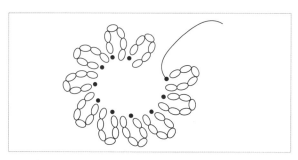

3 Flower centre:

Using beige, *make 6ch, ss in first of 6ch, rep from * until there are 10 loops. Fasten off leaving a 20cm (8in) length of yarn.
Wind the length of loops round to form the centre and sew tog on WS.

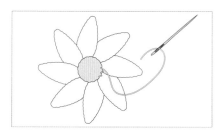

4 Place flower centre in middle of petals and sew securely on WS.

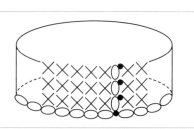

5 Ring:

Using metallic yarn, make 17ch, ss in first ch to form a ring. Number of ch can be adjusted to fit finger.
Round 1 1ch, 1dc in each ch, ss in 1ch.
Round 2 1ch, 1dc in each dc, ss in 1ch.
Round 3 As round 2.
Fasten off.

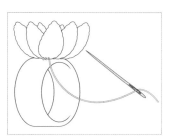

6 Place the flower on the ring covering the ss in each round, and using off-white sew securely in place.

Seven-Petalled Silk Flower Ring

MATERIALS

3mm crochet hook

Silk yarn, beige, off-white

Metallic yarn, gold

This silk flower ring is similar to the project on page 60 but the colours are reversed and there are only seven petals, creating a slightly smaller but still striking design. You could also make the petals in a more brightly coloured yarn as yet another variation.

CROCHET KEY

ss (slip stitch)	•
ch (chain stitch)	O
dc (double crochet)	×
htr (half treble crochet)	T
tr (treble crochet)	T̵
dtr (double treble crochet)	T̵

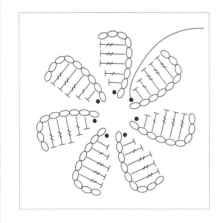

1 Petals:

Using beige, *make 9ch, miss 3ch, 1dtr in each of next 3ch, 1tr in next ch, 1htr in next ch, 1ss in last ch, rep from * until a total of 7 petals have been worked.

Fasten off leaving a 30cm (12in) length of yarn. With WS facing arrange petals to form a circle, overlapping petals. Catch ends tog at centre.

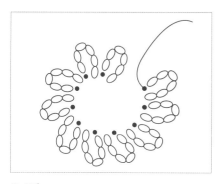

2 Flower centre:

Using off-white, *make 6ch, ss in first of 6ch, rep from * until there are 10 loops. Fasten off leaving a 20cm (8in) length of yarn. Wind the length of loops round to form the centre and sew tog on WS. Place flower centre in middle of petals and sew securely on WS.

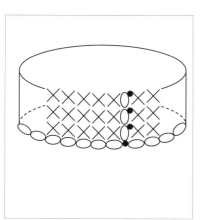

3 Ring:

Using metallic yarn, make 17ch, ss in first ch to form a ring. Number of ch can be adjusted to fit finger.

Round 1 1ch, 1dc in each ch, ss in 1ch.
Round 2 1ch, 1dc in each dc, ss in 1ch.
Round 3 As round 2.
Fasten off.
Place the flower on the ring covering the ss in each round, and using beige sew securely in place.

MATERIALS

2.50mm crochet hook

Pearl cotton embroidery thread
No. 8, pink, beige

One 6mm faceted bead

Six 4mm faceted beads

These rings are made of pink and green cotton
embroidery threads, embellished with your
favourite beads in the centre. Have fun choosing
colours from the huge range available.

CROCHET KEY

ss (slip stitch)   •

ch (chain stitch)   O

dc (double crochet)   ×

htr (half treble crochet) T

tr (treble crochet)   T̄

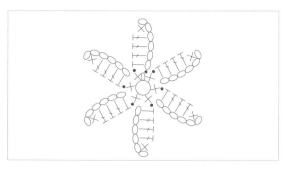

1 Petals:

Using pink, wrap yarn around finger to form a ring.
Round 1 1ch, 6dc in ring, ss in 1ch.
Pull up end to tighten ring.
Round 2 [6ch, 1dc in 2nd ch from hook, 1tr in each of next 3ch, 1htr in last ch, 1ss in next dc of round 1] 6 times.
Fasten off leaving a 30cm (12in) length of yarn.

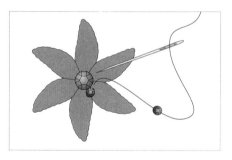

2 With WS facing, catch ends of petals tog, ensuring they meet at centre. With RS facing, sew 6mm bead in centre of flower, then sew six 4mm beads to form a ring around larger bead.

3 Ring:

Using beige, make 17ch, ss in first ch to form a ring.
Number of ch can be adjusted to fit finger.
Round 1 1ch, 1dc in each ch, ss in 1ch.
Round 2 1ch, 1dc in each dc, ss in 1ch.
Round 3 As round 2.
Fasten off.
Place the flower on the ring covering the ss in each round, and using pink sew securely in place.

Eight-Petalled Cotton Flower Ring

MATERIALS

2.50mm crochet hook

Pearl cotton embroidery thread
No. 8, green, beige

6mm faceted bead

Seed beads

Like the Cotton Flower Ring (see page 64), this has the impact of a cocktail ring but in an understated style, so it can be worn everyday.

CROCHET KEY

ss (slip stitch)	●
ch (chain stitch)	O
dc (double crochet)	✕
ttr (triple treble crochet)	⌇

1 Petals:

Using green, wrap yarn around finger to form a ring.
Round 1 1ch, 8dc in ring, ss in 1ch.
Pull up end to tighten ring.
Round 2 [4ch, 1ttr, 4ch, 1ss] in each dc of round 1, ss in first dc of round 1.
Fasten off.

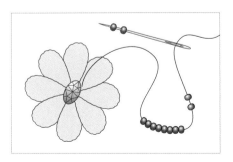

2 With WS facing, catch ends of petals tog, ensuring they meet at centre. With RS facing, sew 6mm bead in centre of flower, then sew seed beads in a circle around larger bead.

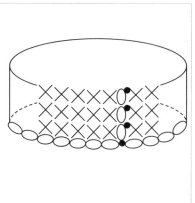

3 Ring:

Using beige, make 17ch, ss in first ch to form a ring.
Number of ch can be adjusted to fit finger.

Round 1 1ch, 1dc in each ch, ss in 1ch.
Round 2 1ch, 1dc in each dc, ss in 1ch.
Round 3 As round 2.

Fasten off.

Place the flower on the ring covering the ss in each round,
and using green sew securely in place (see step 6, page 61).

I made this silk necklace and bracelet for my friend's wedding – she looked very beautiful in a simple and elegant dress with the swinging flowers at her neck and wrist. Whether you make it for yourself or a close friend, sister or daughter, it will be a heartfelt gift that will bring the bride luck and happiness.

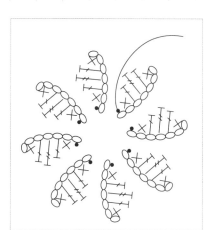

1 Flower A:

*Make 7ch, 1dc in 2nd ch from hook, 1tr in next ch, 1dtr in next ch, 1tr in next ch, 1dc in next ch, 1ss in last ch, rep from until a total of 8 petals have been worked.
Fasten off leaving a 30cm (12in) length of yarn.
With WS facing arrange petals to form a circle, overlapping petals. Catch ends tog at centre.
Make a total of 16 of flower A.

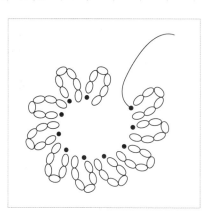

2 Flower centre:

*Make 6ch, ss in first of 6ch, rep from * until there are 10 loops.
Fasten off leaving a 20cm (8in) length of yarn.
Wind the length of loops round to form the centre and sew tog on WS.
Make a total of 16 flower centres.
Sew a flower centre in middle of each flower A.

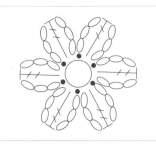

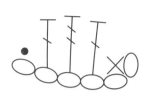

3 Flower B:

Wrap yarn around finger to form a ring.

Round 1 [3ch, 1dtr, 3ch, 1ss in ring]
6 times, ss in first ch.

Fasten off.

Pull up end to tighten ring.

Make a total of 8 of flower B.

4 Leaf:

Make 6ch.

Row 1 1dc in 2nd ch from hook, 1tr in
next ch, 1dtr in next ch, 1tr in next ch, ss
in last ch.

Fasten off.

Make a total of 51 leaves.

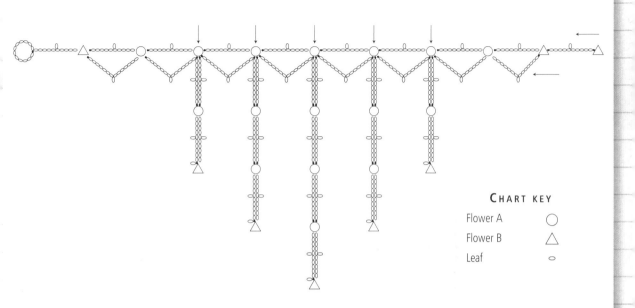

CHART KEY

Flower A	○
Flower B	△
Leaf	○

5 Starting at top right of chart, link flowers and leaves tog with ch.

Top strand Join yarn to WS at centre of a flower B, 10ch, ss in a leaf, 6ch, ss in a flower B, [6ch, ss in leaf, 6ch, ss in flower A] 7 times, 6ch, ss in leaf, 6ch, ss in flower B, 6ch, ss in leaf, 16ch, ss in 10th ch to form fastening loop.
Fasten off.
This completes top strand of chart.

Second strand Starting at right of chart, join yarn to WS at centre of 2nd flower B of top strand, [7ch, ss in leaf, 7ch, ss in WS of flower A of top strand] 7 times, 7ch, ss in leaf, 7ch, ss in WS of flower B of top strand.

Fasten off.
This completes second strand of chart.

First drop Starting at right of chart, join yarn to WS at centre of 2nd flower A of top strand.

First side Working down from top strand, 5ch, ss in leaf, 5ch, ss in flower A, 5ch, ss in leaf, 5ch, ss in flower B.

Second side Working back towards top strand, [ss in leaf, 5ch] twice, ss in back of flower A of first side of drop, 5ch, ss in leaf, 5ch, ss in 2nd flower A on top strand.
Fasten off.
This completes first drop.
Following chart, work remaining 4 drops.

When this bracelet is worn with the Bridal Flower Necklace (see page 68), the two pieces make a stunning set. However, you could also make the bracelet as an individual piece; why not try making it in a different colour to accessorize a daytime or party outfit?

MATERIALS

2.50mm crochet hook

Medium-weight silk yarn,
off-white

CROCHET KEY

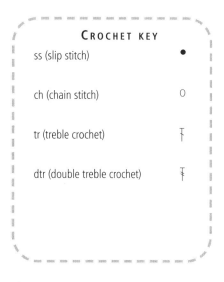

ss (slip stitch)	●
ch (chain stitch)	O
tr (treble crochet)	⊤
dtr (double treble crochet)	⧢

1 Flower A:

Wrap yarn around finger to form a ring.
Round 1 [3ch, 1dtr, 3ch, 1ss in ring] 6
times, ss in first ch.
Fasten off.
Pull up end to tighten ring.
Make a total of 11 of flower A.

2 Flower B:

Wrap yarn around finger to form a ring.
Round 1 [3ch, 1dtr, 3ch, 1ss in ring] 5
times, ss in first ch.
Fasten off.
Pull up end to tighten ring.
Make a total of 11 of flower B.

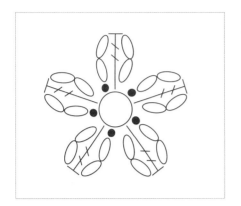

3 Flower fastener:

Wrap yarn around finger to form a ring.
Round 1 [2ch, 1tr, 2ch, 1ss in ring]
5 times, ss in first ch.
Fasten off.
Pull up end to tighten ring.
Make 1 flower fastener.

4 Starting at top left of chart, link flowers tog with ch.

Main chain Join yarn to centre of WS of flower fastener, make 58ch, miss 10ch, ss in next ch to form fastening loop.
Do not fasten off.
Join flowers:

First side *2ch, ss in back of a flower A, 2ch, miss 3ch of main chain, ss in next ch of main chain, 3ch, ss in back of a flower B, 3ch, miss next 3ch of main chain, ss in next ch of main ch, rep from * until 6 of flower A and 5 of flower B have been joined.

Second side Now work back along other side of main ch, noting that each ss is worked into the same ch as a ss on first side. **3ch, ss in back of a flower B, 3ch, miss 3ch of main chain, ss in next ch of main chain, 2ch, ss in back of a flower A, 2ch, miss next 3ch of main chain, ss in next ch of main ch, rep from ** until all flowers have been joined.
Fasten off.

Embellishments

Basic sewing kit

For your pieces of jewellery to have that professional finish, it is worth investing in some good-quality pieces of equipment and mastering a few basic sewing and crochet stitches. Here you will find a guide to sewing-basket essentials, together with instructions for basic techniques to help you get started and stitch references for simple embroidery and crochet stitches.

CHAPTER 3
Equipment, Techniques and Stitch Library

Basic sewing kit

Embellishments

Making cashmere flowers

Making beaded tassels

Making pompoms

Making a ring clasp

Embroidery stitches

Crochet stitches

Tips for beginners

Making beaded
tassels

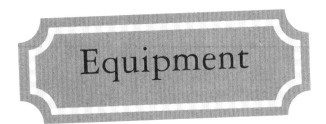

Equipment

If you are new to sewing and crochet, then you will need to furnish your sewing basket with a few basics to get you started. In addition to the simple tools – needles, scissors, tape measure – your choice of yarns and threads will shape your projects, personalizing them with your own colour schemes. Many of the projects can be adapted as necklaces, bracelets, belts and brooches, and you will even be able to create earrings with the appropriate findings.

Basic sewing kit

Always choose the best quality you can afford for reliable and long-lasting tools. You can always supplement your basic kit, and you will soon be adding to your stash of threads, yarns and beads whenever you visit your craft store.

Scissors

You will need dressmakers' scissors or shears for cutting out fabric, together with a pair of small, sharp embroidery scissors for cutting threads and smaller pieces of fabric. Keep a separate pair of scissors for cutting paper or card templates, as paper can blunt the blades, making it difficult to cut fabric accurately.

Needles and pins

Use general sewing needles for stitching seams and embroidery needles for embellishing pieces with embroidery stitches and for threading some of the projects together. Keep pins to hand for holding fabrics in place prior to sewing.

Sewing threads

Cotton sewing threads are available in an infinite variety of colours to match any fabric or yarn. They are suitable for tacking fabrics together prior to sewing or embellishing, and for sewing seams or attaching beads.

Embroidery threads

Available in different counts, embroidery threads have a wonderful, silky texture and appearance that looks beautiful when used for crochet projects and are strong enough to make a necklace chain, whether chain stitched or knotted together with beads. Stranded embroidery thread, a heavier thread, is perfect for adding embellishments and decorative stitches. Pearl cotton thread is particularly suited to crochet projects since it is non-divisible and fairly thin. It comes in three weights: No. 8 (finest), No. 5 and No. 3 (heaviest).

Yarns

Wool yarns have a wonderful warm texture and depth of colour that adds a different dimension to jewellery. Whether used to create fluffy pompoms or crocheted as beads, their characteristics make them very appealing for jewellery work. Other more unconventional yarns can also be used for jewellery, such as lamé (metallic) yarn and raffia yarn. Raffia yarn is available in 25g hanks, and one hank per colour used will be sufficient for each project in this book.

Tape measure

For some projects, accurate measuring is essential. A tape measure or ruler should always be to hand for checking measurements and you should use one system of measurement, imperial or metric, never a mixture of both.

Crochet hooks

Depending on the size, crochet hooks can be made from metal, plastic or wood. Choose a hook that has a smooth point and notch. The instructions for each project give a recommended hook size, but use the conversion chart (see page 80) if required.

Embellishments

In addition to the effects that you can achieve with a needle and thread, you can embellish your work with beads and other decorations that are readily available from your craft store. Choose from cut glass to tiny seed beads and semi-precious stones.

Crochet hook conversions

Metric (mm)	US size	UK/Canada (old) Wool	UK/Canada (old) Cotton
0.60	No. 14 steel	–	7
0.75	No. 12 steel	–	6½
1.00	No. 10 steel	–	5½
1.25	No. 9 steel	–	4½
1.50	No. 8 steel	16	3½
1.75	No. 7 steel	15	2½
2.00	B/1	14	1½
2.50	C/2	12	0
3.00	D/3	11	3
3.50	E/4	9	4
4.00	F/5	8	5
4.50	G/6	7	
5.00	H/8	6	
5.50	I/9	5	
6.00	J/10	4	
6.50	K10½	3	
7.00	K10½	2	
8.00	L/12	0	
9.00	M/13	00	
10.00	N/15	000	
12.00	N/15	000	
15.00	N/15	000	
17.00	N/15	000	
25.00	N/15	000	
35.00	N/15	000	

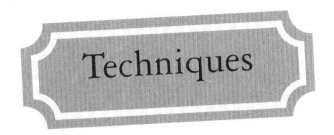
Making cashmere flowers

What better way to make use of beautiful but worn cashmere sweaters than to transform them into delicate little flowers? All your fond memories associated with the sweaters are in the flowers, which can act as stylish wrist-warmers (see page 30) or become an elegant long necklace (see page 32). I find making cashmere flowers very enjoyable work – it's a little like baking cookies using similar techniques to making dough, with an equally sweet end result!

MATERIALS

Embroidery needle

Elastic yarn No. 30 (thick)

Old cashmere sweaters, in
a selection of four different colours

Wash your cashmere sweaters gently – don't worry if they shrink a little. Cut a sweater into its component parts – body, sleeves, hems and cuffs.

Now, cut strips along the edges. The ribs of hems and cuffs are stretchy and work well as the centre of the flowers for cord A.
Cut the strips to the following widths:
Rolled flowers (see page 82):
Centre of flower (cord A): 1.5cm (⅝in) wide
Rolled petals (cord B): 2cm (¾in) wide
Eight-petalled flowers (see page 83):
Centre of flower (cord C): 1.5cm (⅝in) wide
Petals (cord D): 8mm (⅜in) wide

Making rolled cashmere flowers

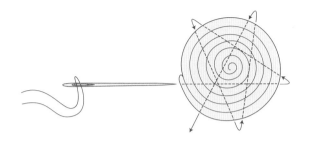

1 Roll a strip of cord A until it measures 1.5cm (¾in) in diameter. Thread a needle with a double length of elastic yarn and push it through the centre of the roll to secure the end. Trim the excess strip.

2 To hold the roll in place, push the needle through in a zigzag pattern, ensuring the threads are pulled taut. The centre of the flower is complete.

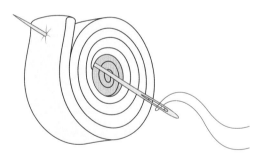

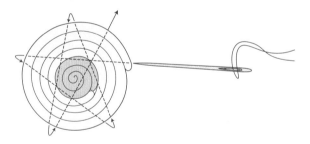

3 Roll a strip of cord B around the centre of the flower until the flower measures 4cm (1½in) in diameter. Trim the excess strip. Push the needle through from the inside of the roll and secure the end of cord B.

4 Push the needle through the whole flower in a zigzag pattern as in step 2, ensuring that the shape of the roll remains round and smooth.

Making eight-petalled cashmere flowers

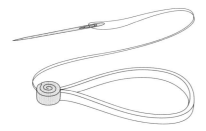

1 Repeat steps 1–2 opposite to make the flower centre using cord C. Cut a 23-cm (9-in) length of cord D and fold it in half lengthways, right sides together. Push the needle through the centre of the end of the strip and the centre of the roll, drawing the thread through.

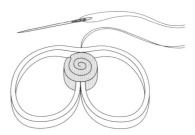

2 Take the needle through the end of the loop of cord D and pull the thread through, drawing the cord against the centre.

3 Take the needle in next to the cord and bring it out on the side opposite a loop in the cord. Pull to tauten. Push the needle through the side of the roll.

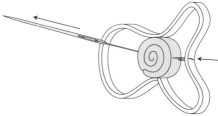

4 Take the needle through from the outside of the cord and back into the centre next to the thread, bringing it out on the opposite side diagonally. Pull to tauten, forming a second petal. Repeat to make four petals.

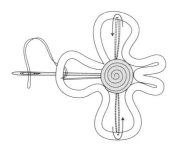

5 Repeat steps 3–4 to make four more of these petals.

6 Knot the thread to complete the flower. Continue to make the required number of flowers for your project.

Making beaded tassels

These tassels are incredibly versatile. They make a bold statement as a bracelet (see page 48) but can also be used to make a ring, necklace or belt, or to decorate a wrap or scarf.

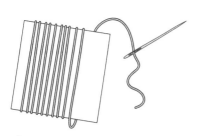

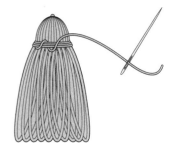

1 Wrap the yarn around a rectangle of stiff card or cardboard, slightly deeper than the required finished pompom diameter. Make 45 wrapped loops around the card.

2 Slip the yarn off the card and wrap the thread end around the top loops several times. Tie tightly to bind the strands together. Leave the long end of thread.

3 In a contrasting colour, if required, wrap yarn around the top of the loops, then stitch over the threads, bringing the needle over and behind the threads to make a stitch. Secure the thread and trim any excess.

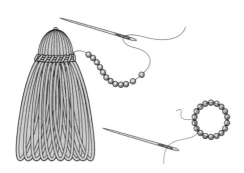

4 To make a beaded tassel, attach a length of beading thread to the top band of yarn. Thread on several small beads to make a full circle around the yarn. Bring the needle back through the first and last two beads to secure together and thread through the tassel to secure in place.

5 Repeat step 4 for the base of the band. Cut the bottom loops of yarn and trim any ends if necessary.

Making pompoms

Pompoms are simple (and very therapeutic!) to make and can be used for all sorts of embellishments, from bracelets (see page 28) and necklaces, to belts, bag charms, brooches and hair clips.

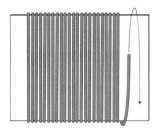

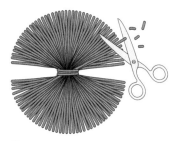

1 Wrap the yarn around a rectangle of stiff card or cardboard, slightly deeper than the required finished pompom diameter. Make 45 wrapped loops around the card.

2 Slip the yarn off the card and wrap a length of matching yarn around the centre, tying tightly. Cut the top and bottom loops of yarn.

3 Fluff out the pompom and neaten any protruding strands.

Making a ring clasp

Several of the necklaces and bracelets in the projects are secured with a clasp made from matching embroidery yarn. Created with a few loops secured with blanket stitch, these are the perfect way to finish your jewellery pieces.

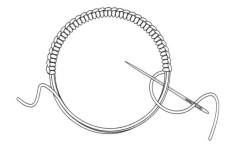

1 Make two or three loops of yarn, and leave the tail end of the yarn.

2 Thread a needle with matching yarn and blanket stitch the loops together (see page 86). To reinforce the ring, pull the tail end of the loop of yarn to bring the stitches together. Secure the thread and trim the excess. The clasp can now be attached to a bracelet or necklace chain.

Stitch Library

Embroidery stitches

There is an incredible range of embroidery stitches at your disposal for decorating your jewellery pieces. Either work them on a base, such as the embroidered flowers on pages 20-27, or use them as added decoration and texture, such as the combinations of French knots and seed beads on the Vibrant Beaded Collar on page 38.

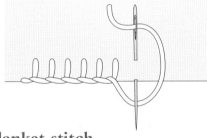

Running stitch
Take several small, even stitches at one time before pulling the thread through.

Blanket stitch
Work from left to right. Bring the thread out on the edge. Insert the needle above and to the right of this point, bringing it out vertically straight down with the thread under the tip of the needle. Pull up the stitch to form the loop and repeat.

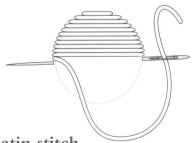

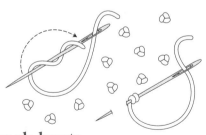

Satin stitch
Work straight stitches closely together across the shape to fill the area required. Keep the edge even and if you are following an outline marked on the fabric, take the stitches outside the line so that the marked line does not show.

French knots
Bring out the needle where you would like to position the knot. Encircle the needle two or three times with the thread, then turn the needle back to reinsert it just above where it first emerged. Holding the thread taut with your left hand or thumb, pull the thread through to the back of the work or bring it up again where you want to position the next stitch.

Crochet stitches

Crochet stitches are all made in a similar way. Apart from slip stitch and chain stitch, the basic crochet stitches vary in height, which is determined by the number of times the yarn is wrapped around the hook.

Crochet is a two-handed craft, with the left hand tensioning the yarn and holding the work while the right hand uses the hook. Because the left hand does a lot of work, most left-handed people find that they are comfortable working this way but if preferred, left-handers could reverse the actions, reading left for right and right for left, using a mirror if necessary to check the illustrations.

Abbreviations

beg	begin(ning)	RS	right side
ch	chain	ss	slip stitch
cm	centimetres	st(s)	stitch(es)
dc	double crochet	tog	together
dtr	double treble crochet	tr	treble crochet
		ttr	triple treble crochet
htr	half treble crochet		
in	inches	WS	wrong side
rep	repeat		

Making a slip knot

A slip knot is needed to start some of the projects. It is not counted as a stitch.

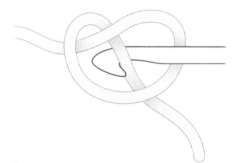

1 Make a loop in the yarn, insert the hook and catch the back strand of the yarn.

Slip stitch

This is the shortest stitch, used for joining stitches, to work to a new place in a pattern or to make a decorative surface chain.

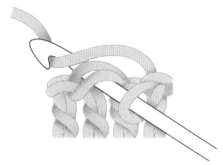

1 Insert the hook into stitch and wrap yarn over hook. Draw a new loop through both the stitch and the loop on the hook, so ending with one loop on the hook.

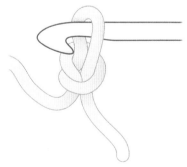

2 Pull a loop through, then gently pull on both ends to tighten the knot and close the loop on the hook.

Chain stitch

Chain stitch may be used as a foundation for other stitches or as a strand to join beads or elements of a necklace.

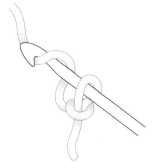

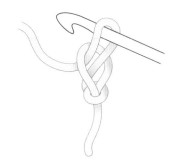

1 With the hook in front of the yarn, dip the tip to take the yarn over the hook from the back to the front and catch the yarn. This is called yarn over hook and is a basic movement for all crochet stitches.

2 Bring the yarn through the loop on the hook to make a new chain loop on the hook.

Double crochet

This is made in the same way as a slip stitch but with an extra stage, giving a stitch that is almost square.

1 Insert the hook into chain or stitch indicated in the instructions, yarn over hook, and draw the yarn through the stitch to make two loops on the hook.

2 Yarn over hook and draw through two loops on hook, so ending with one loop on the hook.

Treble crochet

Wrapping the yarn around before inserting the hook makes a longer stitch.

1 Yarn over hook, insert hook into chain or stitch indicated in the instructions. Yarn over hook, pull through the stitch to make three loops on the hook. Yarn over hook, pull through the first two loops on the hook, so making two loops on the hook.

2 Take the yarn over the hook again and pull through the two loops, so ending with one loop on the hook.

Half treble crochet

This is made in the same way as treble crochet but the stitch is shorter.

1 Work as for treble crochet until there are three loops on the hook. Yarn over hook and draw through three loops on hook, so ending with one loop on the hook.

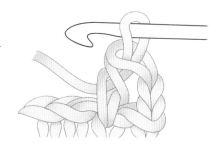

Working longer stitches

Longer stitches are worked in the same way as a treble but with one more wrapping of the yarn around the hook at the start, so giving one more step when drawing through two loops at a time. Work these stitches as follows:

Double treble: Wrap the yarn round the hook twice and insert in the 5th chain from the hook, yarn around hook and pull through so you have four loops on the hook. Take the yarn around the hook again and pull through 2 loops; repeat three times until you are back to one loop on the hook.

Triple treble: Wrap the yarn round the hook three times and insert in the 6th chain from the hook, yarn around hook and pull through so you have five loops on the hook. Take the yarn around the hook again and pull through 2 loops; repeat four times until you are back to one loop on the hook.

Tips for beginners

Working the stitches

If you've never tried using crochet before, use a smooth, medium-weight, light-coloured yarn and a medium-sized hook to try out the basic stitches that are explained on these pages before starting a project.

Holding the hook

Hold the hook like a pencil with the shaft above your hand. Your grip should be light so that you can easily extend the hook in a forwards and back motion.

Holding the yarn

Make a slip knot on the hook, then catch the yarn that goes to the ball around the little finger of the left hand. Bring the hook towards you to take the yarn over the fingers and hold the tail end of yarn from the slip knot between first finger and thumb. Extend the middle finger to make a space for the hook to catch the yarn. As you make stitches, allow the yarn to ease through the fingers and move the work to keep a grip near the place that a new stitch will be made. If working with fine or slippery yarn, wrap the yarn more times around the middle finger.

Templates

All the templates for the projects are given in this section. Follow the instructions as to whether you can to trace them at full-size or need to double their size using a photocopier.

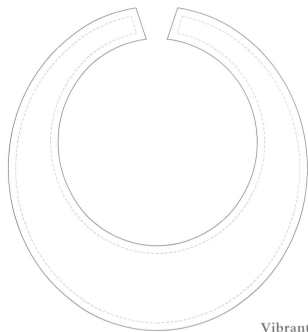

Vibrant Beaded Collar, page 38 (Shown at 50% – enlarge on a photocopier by 200%)

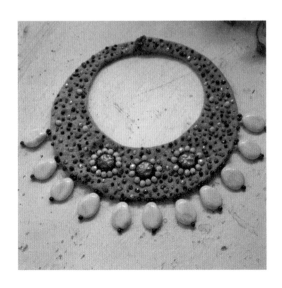

Linen Flower Necklace, page 34
(Shown at 100% – use the templates
at this size)

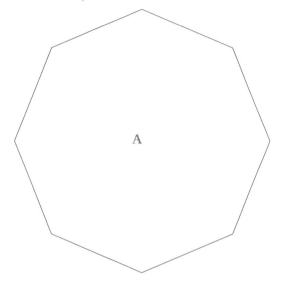

A

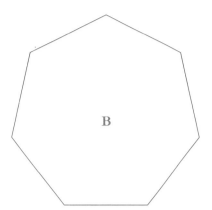

B

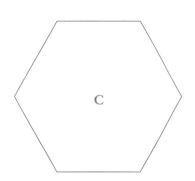

C

LEAF

Linen Flower Hair Clip, page 36 (Shown at 100% – use the templates at this size)

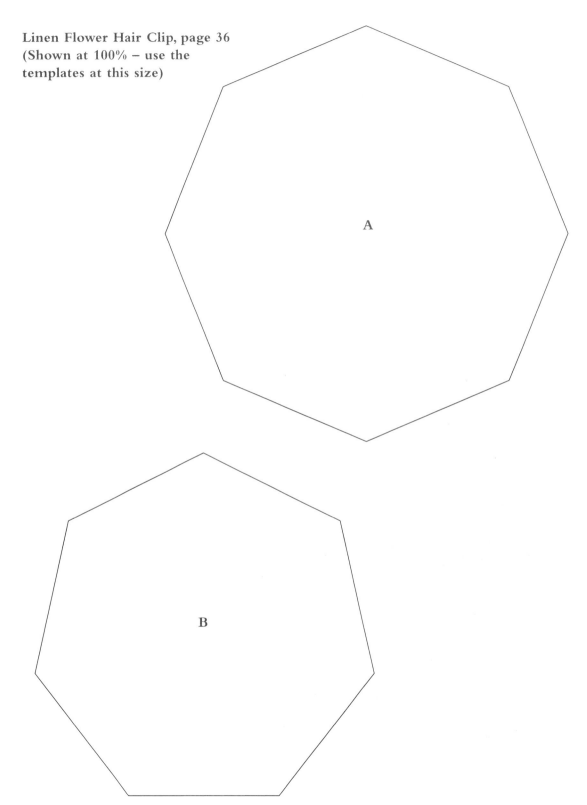

A

B

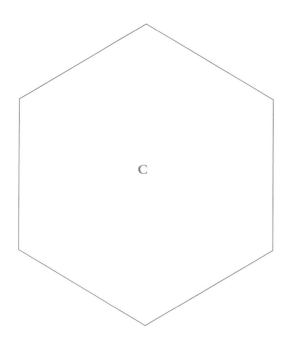

C

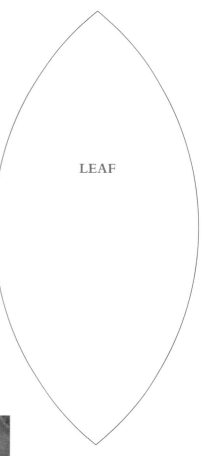

LEAF

Suppliers

Yarns and embroidery threads

DMC (stores worldwide)
www.dmc.com
(Embroidery threads)

Rowan (stores worldwide)
www.knitrowan.com

UK
Coats Crafts
www.coatscrafts.co.uk
(Rowan)

Designer Yarns
www.designeryarns.uk.com
(Debbie Bliss; Noro)

HobbyCraft
www.hobbycraft.co.uk
(DMC embroidery threads)

John Lewis
www.johnlewis.com
(Sirdar)

Sirdar
www.sirdar.co.uk

Australia
Prestige Yarns
www.prestigeyarns.com
(Debbie Bliss; Noro)

Sunspun
www.sunspun.com.au
(Rowan)

New Zealand
Knit World
www.knitting.co.nz
(Rowan)

United States
Knitting Fever
www.knittingfever.com
(Debbie Bliss, Noro; Sirdar)

Canada
Diamond Yarns
www.diamondyarn.com
(Debbie Bliss; Sirdar)

Beads and embellishments

UK
Bead Addict
www.beadaddict.co.uk

Bead Aura
www.beadaura.co.uk

Beads Direct
www.beadsdirect.co.uk

Beadworks Bead Shop
www.beadworks.co.uk

Bijoux Beads
www.bijouxbeads.co.uk

Crystals
www.crystalshop.co.uk

London Bead Company
www.londonbeadco.co.uk

Spangles
www.spangles4beads.co.uk

US
Beadalon
www.beadalon.com

Fire Mountain Gems and Beads
www.firemountaingems.com

Great Craft Works
www.greatcraftworks.com

Marvin Schwab, The Bead Warehouse
www.thebeadwarehouse.com

Phoenix Beads, Jewelry and Parts
www.phoenixbeads.com

Rings and Things
www.rings-things.com

Swarovski
www.swarovski.com

Author's websites

www.car-g-mom.com (in Japanese)

Emi Iwakiri's crochet kits are available from
www.hobbyra-hobbyre.com
(in Japanese)

Index

Acknowledgements

I would like to acknowledge the generosity and kindness of my family, Takashi, my husband, Taisuke, my son, Momo, my daughter and Kiri, my dog, who shared parts of their lives to help me for this book, as well as Katsura, my mother, who encouraged me to explore new opportunities and Kikue, my grandmother, who inspired me with crochet and textile work and gave me all her skills. I really appreciate the help of Michie Takatsuki, who helped me to make the pieces. I am truly grateful to Kei Hirano who loves my work and made this opportunity possible. Big thanks to Cindy Richards for commissioning the book and Becky Maynes for her beautiful photographs. Thanks to Sally Powell and Fahema Khanam for the lovely design, Katie Hardwicke for editing the text and all the wonderful people behind the scenes at CICO Books. This book was made by all of your dedication.